The Massachusetts Colony

Bob Italia
ABDO Publishing Company

visit us at
www.abdopub.com

Published by ABDO Publishing Company, 4940 Viking Drive, Edina, Minnesota 55435.
Copyright © 2001 by Abdo Consulting Group, Inc. International copyrights reserved in all
countries. No part of this book may be reproduced in any form without written permission from
the publisher.

Printed in the United States.

Cover Photo Credit: North Wind Picture Archives
Interior Photo Credits: North Wind Picture Archives (pages 7, 9, 11, 13, 15, 17, 19, 21, 25, 27, 29),
    Corbis (page 23)

Contributing Editors: Tamara L. Britton, Kate A. Furlong, and Christine Fournier
Book Design and Graphics: Neil Klinepier

Library of Congress Cataloging-in-Publication Data

Italia, Bob, 1955-
   The Massachusetts Colony / Bob Italia.
      p. cm. -- (The colonies)
   Includes index.
   ISBN 1-57765-584-2
      1. Massachusetts--History--Colonial period, ca. 1600-1775--Juvenile literature. [1.
Massachusetts--History--Colonial period, ca. 1600-1775.] I. Title. II. Series.

F67 .I85 2001
974.4'02--dc21

                                                              2001018870

Contents

The Massachusetts Colony

Native Americans were Massachusetts's first settlers. They lived there more than 3,000 years ago. Europeans began exploring the coast in 1497.

Pilgrims from England landed on Cape Cod in 1620. They formed the Plymouth Colony. In 1628, the **Puritans** arrived and formed the Massachusetts Bay Colony.

The new colonies governed themselves. The church was the center of each community. The colonists made a living by farming and trading.

The early colonists lived peacefully with the Native Americans until King Philip's War. It was a long and violent war. Many colonists and Native Americans were killed.

After the war, more colonists arrived to start new towns. In the 1700s, the colonists started talking about independence from England.

Many events that led up to the **American Revolution** took place in Massachusetts. Today, Massachusetts is an important part of America's **economy**.

NY

NH

ATLANTIC
OCEAN

NAUMKEAG
RIVER

CAPE ANN

PENNACOOK   o Concord
              o Lexington

o Salem

Massachusetts Bay Colony

MASSACHUSETT ——   o Boston

▲ MT.
GREYLOCK

The
Massachusetts
Colony

POCOMTUC

MASSACHUSETTS
BAY

CAPE
COD

*Plymouth
Colony*

NIPMUC

NAUSET   o Plymouth

WAMPANOAG

o Mashpee

CT

RI

WAMPANOAG

Gay   o
Head   Martha's
        Vineyard

Detail Area

The Thirteen
Colonies

NH

NY

MA

CT

RI

PA

NJ

MD

DE

VA

NC

SC

GA

ATLANTIC
OCEAN

Early Colonial History

Massachusetts is one of the six New England states. The other five are Maine, New Hampshire, Vermont, Connecticut, and Rhode Island.

Massachusetts is made up of hills and valleys. Western Massachusetts has mountains. The highest point is Mount Greylock. It is 3,500 feet (1,100 m) high. From there, the land slopes down to the Atlantic Ocean.

Native Americans lived in present-day Massachusetts more than 3,000 years ago. These **Algonquian**-speaking (al-GON-kwee-an) tribes included the Massachusett, Nauset, Nipmuc, Pennacook, Pocomtuc, and Wampanoag (wahm-puh-NO-ag).

The Wampanoag was the most powerful tribe. Its people farmed, fished, and hunted. They lived in houses called *weetus* (WEE-tooz).

Weetus were built of sapling frames covered with bark and **cattail** mats. Around 1616, a plague struck the Wampanoag and other Native Americans. Many people died.

Many Native Americans in Massachusetts died from diseases brought by European explorers.

The First Explorers

French and Spanish fishermen visited the region during the 1400s. And John Cabot sailed along the Massachusetts coast in 1497 and 1498.

In 1602, Bartholomew Gosnold landed on the Elizabeth Islands. He gave Cape Cod its name. In 1614, Captain John Smith sailed along the coast.

Captain Christopher Jones commanded the *Mayflower*. On November 21, 1620, he brought 102 **Pilgrims** to Cape Cod. Before they left the ship, they wrote the **Mayflower Compact**. It established the new colony's government.

When the *Mayflower* landed at Cape Cod, a group of men explored the area. But there was no fresh water. And the soil was poor. So they continued to explore.

On December 21, they found a good place to settle. They called it Plymouth. It was the first of many settlements in the Massachusetts Colony.

The *Mayflower*

Settlement

Late in 1620, the **Pilgrims** started building Plymouth Colony. Winter was quickly approaching. They had only enough time to build thatched huts and cave houses. They did not have much food and it was too cold to plant crops. The winter of 1620 was long and hard. Only 52 Pilgrims lived until spring.

Slowly, the Massachusetts Colony began to grow. In 1623, England's Dorchester Company started a fishing settlement on Cape Ann. Three years later, Roger Conant started a settlement along the Naumkeag (nahm-keg) River. In 1630, colonists named the settlement Salem.

In 1628, **Puritans** arrived from England. They started the Massachusetts Bay Colony. It was north of the Plymouth Colony. Massachusetts Bay was the largest and most successful early New England colony.

In 1630, Governor John Winthrop brought about 1,000 people to settle the Massachusetts Bay area.

During the 1630s, thousands of Puritans came from England to the Massachusetts Bay Colony. They founded the city of Boston.

In 1643, the Plymouth and Massachusetts Bay Colonies joined with the Connecticut and New Haven Colonies. They formed the United Colonies of New England. It provided safety and a way to solve common problems.

Boston, Massachusetts Bay Colony

Colonial Government

In the Massachusetts Colony, colonists formed the government. It made laws, formed the **militia** (muh-LISH-uh), and punished criminals.

The colony had a governor, a council, and a general court. The general court made laws and heard court cases. It also made agreements with Native Americans and other colonies. By 1639, each settlement had representatives in the general court.

If the colonists broke the law, they were punished. Punishment included being whipped, paying fines, and going to jail.

The militia defended the colony. Every man between the ages of 16 and 60 had to serve in it. The militia met several times a year to practice marching and shooting.

Some laws hurt the colonists. In 1692, the Salem witchcraft trials took place. One hundred fifty people were accused of being witches.

Plymouth Colony's first seal

Nineteen of them were found guilty. According to law, they were hanged.

The witchcraft trials lasted about a year. Then the colony's ministers ended them. They realized the trials were unfair. In 1693, the people still in jail on witchcraft charges were freed.

In 1711, the colony's government made payments to the families of the victims. Witchcraft trials were never again held in America.

A witness testifies at a witchcraft trial in Salem.

Life in the Colony

The **Pilgrims** and **Puritans** in the Massachusetts Colony formed close communities. They had the same religious beliefs. And they governed themselves. They worked together to make their communities successful.

The church was the center of community life. Each church was independent. Its members determined how they practiced religion. They did not support other churches' beliefs. The community's general courts sent nonbelievers away.

Each community had a meetinghouse. It was used for church services. Most people went to church twice a week. The meetinghouse was used for town meetings, too.

The colonists celebrated three kinds of holidays. They were Sabbath days, days of thanksgiving, and fast days. Government leaders proclaimed days of feasting and days of fasting.

In October 1621, the **Pilgrims** celebrated a harvest festival. A Native American named Squanto (SKWAN-tow) had taught them how to grow corn. The corn the colonists planted had grown well. So they celebrated with feasts, games, and prayers. This was the first Thanksgiving.

Pilgrims on their way to church services

Making a Living

The colonists made a living farming and trading. They sent the goods they produced to England. They sent timber and furs to England, too. The colonists also traded goods with the Dutch.

Soon trained craftsmen came to Massachusetts Colony. The first craftsmen were **joiners** and carpenters. The colonists began to make their own furniture and other wooden items. Local styles of furniture and houses began to develop.

Boston craftsmen produced many finished goods. The Saugus (SAW-gus) Ironworks was founded in 1643. It made tools, nails, and **firebacks**. Silversmiths began making coins as early as 1651.

Soon the colonists could buy many kinds of furniture, tools, and clothing. Through England, the colonists could also buy goods from around the world. By the end of the 1600s, people in the Massachusetts Colony had more comfortable lives.

A blacksmith makes an iron tool on an anvil.

Food

The early colonists hunted and gathered food in the forests. They hunted deer, quail, and partridge. Later, they raised cows and pigs. They stored meat in pork barrels.

The forests also supplied the colonists with fruits and nuts. Cherries, gooseberries, strawberries, and plums were plentiful. Colonists also enjoyed walnuts, chestnuts, hickory nuts, and acorns.

Since the colony was on the ocean, the colonists ate much seafood. Fishermen caught lobster, herring, smelt, and eels.

Colonists cooked meals in the large kitchen fireplace. They boiled food in kettles. They cooked meat on an iron spit. As the spit turned, it roasted the meat evenly on all sides.

Colonists cooked potatoes and eggs in the fireplace ashes. They wrapped the food in wet leaves, and covered it in hot coals. Colonists baked bread and other foods, such as squash and pumpkins, in brick ovens.

Native Americans taught the settlers how to plant, raise, and prepare corn. Hominy, pone, samp, and succotash became diet staples. Colonists also ground corn into flour to use in bread.

Colonists drank apple cider. Nearly every farm had a cider mill. Cider was the colony's most common drink.

A colonist cooks food in her home's large fireplace.

Clothing

At first, the early colonists had to buy their clothes from England. But soon farmers grew their own flax. They also raised sheep for wool.

Flax is a plant with long, silklike fibers in its stem. The women spun flax fibers and wool into yarn on a spinning wheel. Then they wove the yarn into cloth on a handloom.

Colonists dyed the cloth different colors using local plants. Blue, red, green, brown, and purple were common colors. Then they cut the cloth and made clothes.

Women wore dresses. They also wore vests and aprons. Men wore linen shirts, long-sleeved tight-fitting jackets called doublets, breeches, and kneesocks. Girls and boys wore dresses until they were about eight years old. Then they wore the same clothes as the adults.

Colonists also made clothes from tanned leather. Shoes were made of leather, too. Colonists with enough money could buy shoes with leather heels. Poorer colonists had shoes with wooden heels.

A woman reads while spinning fiber into yarn.

Homes

The early colonists lived in tents, caves, and wigwams (WIG-wahmz). Wigwams were made of sapling frames covered with grass mats.

To make a cave, colonists dug a hole in the ground about 7 feet (2 m) deep. They used logs to make the walls stronger, and filled the spaces between the logs with bark. They covered the hole with a wooden frame covered with bark or sod.

Colonists lived in these shelters until they could build thatched homes. Later, when lumber became available, they built clapboard houses.

Most colonists built one-room houses. When a family grew larger, it added more rooms to the house. At one end of the house was a large fireplace. Colonists used it for cooking, heating, and lighting. They also lit their homes with candles.

Many houses had small windows because of the cold climate. Some colonists could afford glass for their windows. Others used oiled paper instead.

A thatched house

Children

Most colonists had families of seven or eight children. Mothers raised the babies and young children. Fathers taught religion to their families.

Reading was important for understanding the Bible. So most children learned to read at home.

Children did not have much time to play. At the age of six or seven, they began to work with their parents. Girls did housework with their mothers. Boys worked with their fathers in the field or the workshop.

Some children went to school. Massachusetts Colony's leaders thought it was important to educate citizens. America's first public high school opened in Boston in 1635. It was called the Boston Latin School. In 1636, Harvard University opened. It was America's first college.

In 1647, the government said that towns with more than 50 citizens must hire a teacher to teach children reading and writing. Towns with more than 100 citizens also had to set up **grammar schools**.

Colonial children in a one-room schoolhouse

Native Americans

Native Americans first met the **Pilgrims** in 1621. Wampanoag men named Samoset (SAM-oh-seht) and Squanto welcomed them. They helped the Pilgrims adjust to their new home.

But soon the colonists and the Wampanoag began to disagree. Colonists wanted to own Wampanoag land. But the Wampanoag thought everyone should share the land.

A man named Metacom (mee-ta-com) led the Wampanoag. The colonists called him King Philip. He wanted to take Wampanoag land back from the colonists.

In 1675, land disagreements led to a war between the colonists and the Wampanoag. It was called King Philip's War. It began in a town called Swansea. The fighting spread to the Connecticut and New Hampshire Colonies.

The war ended in 1676. Many people on both sides died. But the Wampanoag did not get their land back. And hundreds of Native Americans were forced to be slaves and servants.

Today, more than 3,000 Wampanoag live in southern Massachusetts. Most live in four communities. They are Gay Head on Martha's Vineyard, Mashpee on Cape Cod, Assonet near Fall River, and Herring Pond near Plymouth.

Metacom, known by the colonists as King Philip

The Road to Statehood

Throughout the 1660s, the English government allowed the American colonies to govern themselves. But after King Philip's War, King James II ordered changes to the colonial governments.

In 1692, Plymouth Colony joined the Massachusetts Bay Colony. Then the Massachusetts Colony became the **Commonwealth** of Massachusetts. In 1695, the New England colonies received new **charters**.

Many of the events that led to the **American Revolution** took place in Massachusetts. These include the **Boston Massacre** in 1770 and the **Boston Tea Party** in 1773.

On April 18, 1775, Paul Revere made his famous ride to warn colonists that England's troops were coming. On April 19, 1775, minutemen at Lexington and Concord fought the first battles of the American Revolution. The colonists won the war.

On February 6, 1788, Massachusetts approved the U.S. **Constitution**. It became the sixth state to join the Union.

Today, Massachusetts is an important part of America's **economy**. Boston is a major U.S. port. And it is New England's trade center. Boston is also one of America's leaders in education and medicine. Massachusetts's rich colonial history makes it one of America's main tourist attractions.

Paul Revere's ride

TIMELINE

1400s - French and Spanish fishermen explore the Massachusetts area
1497 - John Cabot explores Massachusetts's coast
1602 - Bartholomew Gosnold lands on Elizabeth Islands
1614 - John Smith explores the coast
1616 - Plague kills many Native Americans
1620 - Pilgrims start Plymouth Colony
1621 - Harvest festival is the first Thanksgiving
1623 - Dorchester Company starts settlement on Cape Ann
1626 - Roger Conant starts settlement on Naumkeag River
1628 - Puritans start Massachusetts Bay Colony
1630 - Settlement at Naumkeag River renamed Salem; John Winthrop brings 1,000 settlers to Massachusetts Bay Colony
1635 - Boston Latin School opens
1636 - Harvard University opens
1643 - United Colonies of New England formed; Saugus Ironworks opens
1647 - Education law passes
1675 - King Philip's War begins; ends the next year
1692 - Salem witchcraft trials; Plymouth and Massachusetts Bay Colonies join to form the Commonwealth of Massachusetts
1770 - Boston Massacre
1773 - Boston Tea Party
1775 - Paul Revere's ride; American Revolution begins
1788 - Massachusetts becomes the sixth state

Glossary

Algonquian - a family of Native American languages spoken from Labrador, Canada, to the Carolinas and westward into the Great Plains.

American Revolution - 1775-1783. A war for independence between England and its colonies in North America. The colonists won and created the United States.

Boston Massacre - on March 5, 1770, English soldiers fired into a crowd of Boston colonists, killing five people.

Boston Tea Party - on December 16, 1773, about 60 Boston colonists, dressed as Native Americans, boarded a ship in Boston Harbor and threw a shipment of tea overboard to protest the Stamp Act of 1765.

cattail - a tall, reed-like water plant with a brown, furry tip.

charter - a written contract that states a colony's boundaries and form of government.

commonwealth - a nation, state, or other political unit, governed by the people for the common good.

Constitution - the laws that govern the United States.

economy - the way a colony, state, or nation uses its money, goods, and natural resources.

fireback - a cast-iron plate that lines the back wall of a fireplace.

grammar school - a high school with an advanced course of study that prepares students for college.

joiner - a person who makes things such as furniture by joining together pieces of wood.

Mayflower Compact - a document, signed by 41 male passengers of the *Mayflower,* that was the foundation of the Plymouth Colony's government.

militia - citizens trained for war and emergencies.

Pilgrims - a group of people who wanted to separate from the Church of England because they thought it needed many changes.

Puritans - a group of people who thought the Church of England needed some changes, but wanted to stay in it.

Web Sites

Plimoth-on-Web   http://www.plimoth.org
This is the official Plimoth Plantation site. Learn about the early Massachusetts Colony and read about the everyday lives of the Pilgrims and the Wampanoag.

Salem, Massachusetts   http://www.salem.org
This is the official site of Salem, Massachusetts. Learn about Salem's history, read about the witchcraft trials, and explore Salem's local attractions.

These sites are subject to change. Go to your favorite search engine and type in Massachusetts Colony for more sites.

Index